MANAGING STRESS AND ANXIETY IN UNCERTAIN TIMES

How to Recognize, Analyze, and Safely Verbalize Your Stress

RUSS CHERRY

CONTENTS

COMING SOON!

ANXIETY IS ONLY DANGEROUS WHEN IT'S STORED OR IGNORED.

THE BEGINNING OF THE ANXIETY BUCKET

I thought I was over it.

I survive cancer. Not survived. Survive. I use the present tense with purpose. Surviving is not a hobby: it's my full-time job.

I survived my first cancer in 1987 when I was just 16 years old. It was Hodgkin's Disease Stage 1A; a cancer that starts in the lymph nodes. It may sound odd when I say this, but it's pretty much the best cancer diagnosis ever. In fact, if you're going to have cancer, this is the best one to have.

I survived my second cancer in 1988. I was 17, and the diagnosis was Stage 4D lung cancer.

Even now, there is nothing beyond Stage 4D except death. In fact, when my oncologist told my parents and I the diagnosis he told me that there was nothing that could be done. He instead suggested we should plan my funeral and call to invite the speakers before dinner because I might not be conscious much longer. "Take him home," he told my parents. "Take him home to die."

It wasn't my best day. It also, despite my doctor's suggestion, was far from being my last day.

I promise I will tell you the whole story…eventually. For now, I will tell you this: miracles happen. After eight months of brutal chemotherapy, my x-rays came back clean. The doctor congratulated me and wished me well. He said that if I lived five years beyond that point they would consider me cured.

By 1993 I was still alive. I was considered cured. At long last, I thought I was over it.

But I wasn't.

Living 20 years past the date of my clean bill of health was the goal I set for myself. (Hey—when you're in your 20s, making it into your 40s seems virtually impossible whether you've had cancer or not!) By 2008, I was still going strong, despite a few debilitating side effects due to the treatments I'd undergone in my teens. I was married to an amazing woman, had two great kids and was doing a job I loved. Everybody said I was one of the happiest guys they'd ever met.

I was speaking to a large oncology department at a regional hospital—a unit considered to be the best in a four-state area. They were impressive at every level, and it was an honor when I was invited to share my story with them. My goal was to help them see how amazingly far cancer treatments had progressed since the dark ages (i.e., the 1980s).

Part of my cancer story includes a bone marrow biopsy. To this day, that biopsy was the most painful experience of my lifetime both physically and emotionally. At the same time, I treasure that experience because of what it taught me. As such, I decided to share it at the end of my presentation.

I walked them through my biopsy, moment by moment, as experienced by a skinny, scared 17-year-old boy. As I began to detail the excruciating pain I felt, you could have heard a pin drop. Until "he" spoke.

"He" was a male nurse, who decided in that moment to share his own experience.

"Come on," he said, his tone matching the roll of his eyes. "It doesn't hurt that bad. I've assisted on countless biopsies. It's a quick procedure, and not as dramatic as you're making it out to be."

The needle they used in my bone marrow biopsy is over six inches long. I know its length, because I still have that needle in my possession. Its barrel is wider than the ink barrel of a ballpoint pen, and the physician must first make an incision with a scalpel before it is used because the needle itself would cause too much damage.

I have—quite literally—seen people faint when they've seen it and heard my story. Others become sick to their stomach, and a number of them will cry. But to this man, it meant nothing.

In that moment, I lost touch with reality. The emotions of 20 years flooded my entire system with a ferocity for which I was completely unprepared. I couldn't think. I could only feel.

I walked towards him with that needle in my hand, unable to take my eyes off of him. The rage I was feeling pounded in my ears. My arm was fully extended, and the needle was soon a few feet from his face. Only a table separated us.

"Have YOU ever had to endure this procedure?" I demanded, seething with contempt. I was shaking. "Have you?" I yelled, my voice resounding. "Have you ever had to endure it—especially from an uncaring nurse like you?"

That's when I saw the look on his face, and what I saw startled me. As I slowly became aware of my surroundings again, I realized he wasn't the only concerned person in the room. The body language of his coworkers spoke volumes.

I stepped back quickly and dropped the hand holding the needle to my side. I apologized and tried to explain what came over me. I didn't want to harm him and I didn't mean to threaten him. In truth, I had no idea what had just happened.

The unit administrator, for whom I will be forever grateful, pulled me aside when my presentation was over. "Have you ever talked with anyone regarding your unresolved anxiety over cancer?" she asked gently.

The thought had never crossed my mind. In the 1980s nobody talked about their cancer experience and "normal" people like me had never heard of unresolved anxiety.

"You need some help," she said.

For the first time in years I was speechless.

She did more than take time to listen to my story—for the first time, someone asked me about how I felt about my experience. Then she put me in touch with a group that works with brand new cancer survivors.

When I was going through chemotherapy at 17, I'd wanted to meet a survivor. Too often I'd felt as if I was the only one who'd ever had to face a Stage 4 diagnosis or have a bag of poison plugged into my arm. Meeting a survivor, I thought, would have given me hope. For some reason, however, I'd never had the chance to do it.

Thanks to this thoughtful administrator I got to be, and still get to be, that guy for several survivors. After more than two decades, I finally found purpose and meaning in what I went through.

That's when the anxiety began to dissipate. It's also when my journey began.

I needed to understand—craved to understand—what I had taken my first steps toward learning. Miracles happen (get used to hearing this phrase from me) and a true friend and mentor came into my life at exactly the right time.

He helped me to realize that all of us have an *Anxiety Bucket*. Every time we get anxious we put a drop or two of anxiety into our buckets. Those buckets, however, only hold so much. When it's filled right to the brim, someone always comes along and puts that one last drop in our buckets.

When they put that one last drop in our bucket do we give them just one drop back?

NO! We give them the whole bucket! And after we have emptied the whole bucket on them we hit them on the side of their head with the bucket to make sure they got the message!

I have also discovered anxiety is a perfectly normal emotion that can influence positive behaviors in my life. When I use my anxiety bucket as a tool - not a reservoir - I have positive outcomes in my life.

The Anxiety Bucket is my attempt to share with you what I learned from my mentor. It's about how unresolved anxiety can diminish your life and how you can manage your anxiety in a healthy way.

Let's get started.

HOW DID ANXIETY GET SUCH A BAD NAME?

When you were a child, you undoubtedly threw a temper tantrum or two. You tossed a toy, you yelled at another kid, you plopped right down in the middle of the grocery store aisle and kicked your feet—you get the picture.

So what did you learn about anxiety? Many of us were told by our parents that anxiety was wrong. Maybe you were even told it was a sin against scripture or even against God Himself.

Perhaps one of the following exchanges happened:

Dad: "You will not be anxious with your mother!"

You: *"Too late. Now what?"*

Mom: "You cannot stay in this room with the rest of us while you're anxious!"

You: *"So if I get anxious, I'm not welcome here? You don't want me?"*

Teacher: "You should look in a mirror right now! You should just see how awful you look when you get anxious!"

| **You:** | *"Anxiety is ugly. I'm ugly. I feel bad enough about the way I look—I don't need that too!"* |

Did you notice that it was okay for the adults to be anxious but not children? Think about the irony of it: anxious adults telling you that you shouldn't be anxious.

As we grow up many of us hear and begin to believe that when we are anxious we are bad. Not what we're doing is bad, but WE are bad. Bad children, bad siblings, bad people. In turn, we learn to express—or not express—our anxiety in various ways. The most common ways I call "The Fearsome Five".

THE FEARSOME FIVE

Ah, the Fearsome Five. Some of the world's most common and remarkably unhealthy ways we humans have found to deal with anxiety. They're as old as man himself: Repression, Suppression, Projection, Diffusion and Misplacement. See if you recognize any of them in yourself or in those around you:

REPRESSION

Repressing anxiety begins by acting as if we aren't anxious. Eventually, we don't even know when we're anxious. Impossible, you might say. Not only possible, I'd respond, but it happens all the time.

Russ: "There have been a lot of changes around here, and it looks like the amount of work you're expected to do has doubled. Does it make you anxious?"

Harold: "Doesn't make me anxious. Doesn't bother me at all. I haven't been anxious since I've been here."

Harold's not lying—he's not even aware of how much anxiety he's repressing. But I guarantee you everyone else does because of the way he behaves when he's not even thinking about it. That's classic repression. He's completely out of touch!

SUPPRESSION

When someone suppresses anxiety, they are well aware of just how anxious they are, but they're not going to tell anyone.

Russ: "There have been a lot of changes around here, and it looks like the amount of work you're expected to do has doubled. Does it make you anxious?"

Harold: "It burns me up!"

Russ: "You should say something."

Harold: "I will not say a word. I won't give them the satisfaction. I'm going to sit here, have an ulcer, a migraine, a stroke and die but I will not tell them!"

People who suppress their anxiety are often thought to be the world's nicest people. You could hit them with your car, but when you die they'll be the first in line at your funeral to say nice things about you. And they'll keep right on doing it until they either drop dead of a heart attack or go ballistic when they just can't take it anymore.

PROJECTION

Sometimes when we try to shut our anxiety down we project it; in other words, instead of saying you are anxious, you'll tell me I am.

Russ: "There have been a lot of changes around here, and it looks like the amount of work you're expected to do has doubled. Does it make you anxious?"

Harold: "Well, it doesn't bother me at all. But, I know two people— maybe three—that are really anxious. Not me personally but I can tell you they are. They've even said they might quit."

Who is Harold really talking about? Himself! And he's not the only one who does it. Projection is everywhere, from high school hallways to the highest offices of government.

DIFFUSION

When an individual engages in diffusion, they say that they are anxious about some large group or entity or thing.

Russ: "There have been a lot of changes around here, and it looks like the amount of work you're expected to do has doubled. Does it make you anxious?"

Harold: "Of course it does! I'm mad at the whole world and everyone in it!"

Russ: "I didn't know that you knew all seven billion people on the planet."

Harold: "I hate them all! Even if I don't know them. This is hate everybody day!"

Hating the whole world keeps Harold from having to focus on what he's really anxious about. That's why people say they hate football teams and owners of global companies and the government. The truth is, however, that every time we blame something larger than life, we almost always have a picture of someone or something very specific in our mind. We just aren't aware of it.

MISPLACED

This is the scariest, most dangerous and most powerful of all five unhealthy responses to our anxiety. Why? Because we are anxious with one person but unload on someone else.

You know the cycle. Boss yells at employee. Employee goes home and yells at his significant other. She unloads on the kids. The kids go out and kick the dog. The dog, who was just taking a nap, needs to respond. The next morning he sees the boss and bites his ankle on the way to work and the cycle starts all over again!

Notice that in this cycle everyone chooses a *safe target*! I did not say right target or correct target. The term is *safe target*. It happens at work and at home. Anxious people are looking for a "safe place" to unload their anxiety. And by "safe", I mean someone who they anticipate won't—or can't—fight back.

Domestic violence, including the abuse of spouses, children and even pets, are grounded in misplaced anxiety. Those who are anxious lack a healthy problem solving paradigm. They are unpredictable and irrational.

Misplaced anxiety is more than taking your anxiety out on someone else. In many situations it can also result in taking out your anxiety on yourself. It often starts with name calling ("I'm an idiot! What as I thinking? I'm so stupid. I'm such a fool.")

WHAT HAPPENS WHEN WE DON'T MANAGE OUR ANXIETY?

When people don't deal with our anxiety, there are natural—and at times unavoidable—consequences. Anxiety can build to the point at which people may cheat, lie, steal and commit crimes. They may physically attack or injure one another. They may even injure themselves.

I am not a psychologist or a licensed counselor, but I have worked with thousands of individuals and groups over the last 20 years. Based on that experience, I will tell you that it is my personal belief that much of the emotional depression people deal with is directly correlated to unresolved anxiety.

To be clear: I'm not talking about those who have clinical depression tied to biological factors. I'm talking about individuals who are frequently sad, frustrated and unable to express what it is that is bothering them. They may also exhibit behaviors such as being late on a frequent/regular basis, forgetting those things they normally remember or making mistakes in tasks they can usually complete without significant errors.

That's why it's critical that we first learn to redefine what anxiety is and then focus on the right ways to address it.

THE FIRST STEP: REDEFINING ANXIETY

Grab a dictionary off your shelf or head online and look up the definition for the word anxiety. What you'll find is that anxiety is both a noun (a feeling) and a verb (an action). Now that fact is important in the great scheme of life, but in terms of *The Anxiety Bucket*, I want you to redefine it.

ANXIETY IS A TEACHER

Anxiety will teach you more about yourself than any other emotion you possess. If you tell me what makes you anxious, I will tell you your moral and ethical code. I will also tell you what matters to you. Here's why: You will not get anxious about things that do not matter to you.

When I'm working with people who get shut down, one of my first questions is what, if anything, makes them anxious. If I can discover that one thing—or that group of things, as the case may be--I have a very good chance of helping them identify what they are missing. Together, we can then work to fill that need and resolve that anxiety.

ANXIETY IS YOUR FRIEND

Don't get me wrong: you and I both know people for whom anxiety is an enemy because of the way they use it. The decisions they make or actions they take as a result of anxiety lead them precisely where they shouldn't go.

But anxiety, like all emotions, is a gift. It is designed to be our friend, to help us know that we are being threatened or that something we value, want or need is at risk.

See if this scenario sounds familiar: You see someone coming towards you who treated you poorly in the past. Perhaps he was a bully in high school or she was a stab-you-in-the-back workmate. Naturally, your anxiety kicks in, saying, "I'd watch out! He fooled you last time. I don't think he should fool you again." It's acting to protect you from that person who has caused you pain—precisely what a good friend does.

ANXIETY IS EUPHORIC

Euphoria is a joyful emotion, so you may be shaking your head at the thought anxiety can play any role in it. But I can give you an example to which most of us can relate.

You're sitting in a group of people. Perhaps it's a business meeting, a classroom or even a restaurant. Someone disagrees with you, perhaps even shows some aggression in making his or her point. You become anxious, but handle the conflict in a healthy way that ultimately leaves the two of you parting as friends.

How do you feel? You feel amazing! You feel, in fact, euphoric! The genesis of that euphoria, however, was anxiety. It was what gives you the energy to drive what you are now feeling.

THE ANXIETY CYCLE

As a child I clearly remember my father telling me that there were bears in the woods. He would say it as we drove through the mountains. He would remind me of it as we went camping. He taught me how to minimize my exposure to bears, how to trek through and live in bear territory. He demonstrated what to do if a bear attacked.

Mentally, I understood everything he said. I kept that checklist in the "When Bears Attack" file folder in my brain. I used the principles he taught me every time I ventured into the wilderness.

Then I ran into a bear.

A real bear! There it was in front of me, a few hundred feet away and just uphill from my position on the trail.

And that's when I realized…

…my father never taught me what I would *feel* when I crossed paths with this bear, and I wasn't prepared for how that threat felt.

Now in fairness to my furry friend, it was only a perceived threat. The bear could attack but he hadn't yet. The feeling, however, was the same.

I felt fear. Gut wrenching, paralyzing fear. A primary emotion that's always there, influencing us, but one we may forget about or not even know exists until the moment it arises.

But then a secondary emotion kicked in. One that was completely unexpected, and one that may surprise you: **Anxiety**.

You see, our friend and teacher Anxiety gives us the energy to respond to threats, and my body absolutely needed to respond. Human biology, in fact, demands it and gives us two options: fight or flight.

Here's what it all looks like:

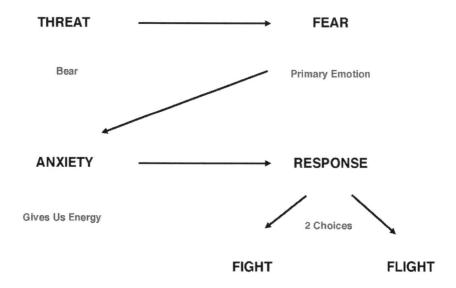

So I see the threat (the bear). I experience the primary emotion of fear. I then become anxious, giving me energy and driving me to respond by either staying and fighting or running away.

The moment I encountered the bear, my adrenaline kicked in. My muscles tightened up. My blood pressure went through the roof! It felt like time slowed down. My body was getting ready to respond to the bear, and I was waiting (not long) for him to make his move.

My mind, in nanoseconds, determined how I would respond.

OPTION ONE: FIGHT

I could fight the bear. Tear into him ferociously, gouge his eyes, claw, scratch, bite, yell, slug, tear, slash, shoot—whatever it would take to win. I would fight in a way that I never had fought and would never be able to fight again. I wouldn't feel the pain of his bite or claws tearing into me. I would be totally focused and fight like a mad man. I'd fight so hard the bear would give up and walk away.

OPTION TWO: FLIGHT

I could run away from the bear, faster than I'd ever run before. I'd climb a tree—the tallest tree—scampering up it like monkey and paying no mind to the scratches or bruises it would leave on my skin. I would scale it in seconds, completely disregarding my technique and scaring the birds that were perched on the branches as I flew by them. That bear wouldn't dream of catching me, so he'd eventually just wander back down the trail.

Either way, I was going to survive the threat! I'd be arms-outstretched-cue-the-dramatic-tune-freakin' King of the World!

Obviously, as you are reading this book, the bear did not prevail in this story. As it turns out, I didn't have to go in swinging or run like the wind—the bear's own fight or flight response and subsequent analysis led him to determine that he could continue on his path without taking the time out of his otherwise busy schedule to deal with me.

But what this experience, and others like it, taught me is that positive outcomes can result from utilizing our natural emotions—including anxiety—properly.

That's where the first Bucket Rule comes in to play.

RULE ONE

A few pages back, we talked about our childhood experiences, those moments we all remember when we were criticized for our anxiety. As a result of these types of experiences, you may have begun to internalize the concept that anxiety naturally leads to punishment.

Your parents got anxious, you got punished. Your teacher got anxious, you got punished. Your friends got anxious, you got punished.

The correlation between feelings of anxiety and the resulting punishment seem clear. So what did you learn about anxiety? To hide it! To put it away. ***To believe the emotion of anxiety is negative.***

But for most of us, we weren't being punished for *feeling* anxiety. We were being punished for our anxious *behavior*.

Let me be clear: It is not the emotion of anxiety, but the behaviors we exhibit while we are anxious that are—or can be—negative. How we use our anxiety is what is most critical.

That's why the second Bucket Rule was established.

RULE TWO
ALL FEELINGS ARE ACCEPTABLE. NOT ALL BEHAVIORS ARE ACCEPTABLE.

I give you permission: You can feel any way you want to, anywhere you want to.

Why do I give you that permission? Because you're going to do it anyway! You get to decide if you're happy about the changes at work or if you want to take a test at school or if you want to be mad at your spouse. Go ahead. Feel away!

HOWEVER, you don't get to behave any way you want to. Your behavior could harm you or other people. It has consequences. And you need to accept, right now, that you can control your behavior.

I challenge you to memorize and apply the following statement into your life as it applies to feelings and behaviors:

> *I will never again apologize for my anxiety.*
> *However, I may have to apologize for my behavior.*

Let's be honest with one another: I have had to apologize for my behavior on more than one occasion since incorporating Bucket Rule #2 into how I live my life. As imperfect humans, all of us have been known to act when we should have been thinking.

In those times, however, I apologized for ***what I did and not for what I felt*** because what I felt informed me that something was bothering me. Unfortunately, I did not pay attention to my feelings and express myself in a healthy way. I didn't take time to think.

THINK

We've now established that anxiety is a **normal**, healthy emotion. Human beings need to respond to things in their environment that make them anxious. It's when we shut those feelings down or misplace them that we get ourselves into trouble. That means it is **necessary** to work through those feelings to get the outcomes that we seek in our lives.

At this point in the book it is important to remind ourselves of a few things by taking another look at the anxiety cycle:

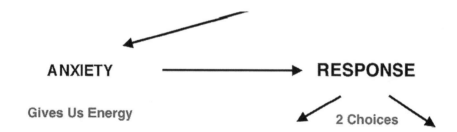

THREAT: We are surrounded by threats every day, all day long. There is nothing we can do about threats.

FEAR: Fear is a primary emotion. Like anxiety, it is normal and necessary. There is nothing we can do about fear.

ANXIETY: Anxiety is the secondary emotion that automatically kicks in when we experience fear. It is a part of our

DNA, and there is nothing we can or should do to eliminate it because it **has the potential** to prompt a healthy response.

RESPONSE: We are going to respond to our emotions. Our bodies, our systems, our emotions demand it! But there is something that we can do about it.

Remember, anxiety is a feeling. All feelings are okay. How we choose to respond will lead to our behaviors. Whether or not that behavior is a healthy productive one hinges on one thing. After the feeling (ANXIETY) but, before the behavior (RESPONSE) we're going to do something. It's a new concept for the 21st Century I hope will catch on.

It's called THINK.

ANXIETY ⟶ [THINK] ⟶ RESPONSE

As we review the anxiety cycle we see that there isn't much that we can do up to and through anxiety but we can THINK *after* we have the feeling and *before* we respond. One rule to remember, however:

Most of us were taught to think as children, although we may not have recognized it as such. When we got anxious we were supposed to count to ten, and the reason we were taught to count to ten was so that we could cool off enough to think and respond in a more socially appropriate way.

Unfortunately, the more anxious we are the harder it is to think, so counting to ten didn't usually work. Once we hit that magical number, our emotion didn't disappear—it just went deeper inside. We would end up with a nervous stomach or a migraine headache or feeling depressed. Or we lashed out like the bully in my school: he'd count to ten and then punch me in the face. He followed the rules, doing what his mother said, but he still beat me up anyway.

My suggestion is that we all stop counting to ten. Instead, may I suggest we count the three steps that can take us from anxiety…to thinking…to healthy response. They are: **recognize**, **analyze**, and **verbalize**.

HOW FULL IS YOUR BUCKET?
(RECOGNIZE)

MILD IRRITATION TO MURDEROUS RAGE

Let's think about our Anxiety Bucket for a minute. As a reminder, most of us carry around a bucket that is usually half-full to seconds away from overflowing. Waking up on a Monday morning ticks most of us off! But by the time we recognize it as anxiety, our chance of dealing with it in a healthy way is very low.

Let's put anxiety on a scale from 1 to 100. We will call our anxiety at level 1 *mild irritation*. Our anxiety at level 100 will be *murderous rage.*

Most of us deal with our anxiety really well up until about 20—which is generally when we notice we are annoyed. However, most of us will not **call** it anxiety until it hits about 80. This isn't a good thing; in fact, it sets the stage for responding in a way you're likely to regret.

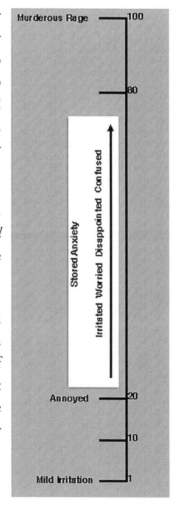

I've had people tell me, "Russ, I know when I'm worked up. I absolutely know when I'm upset".

I agree with them, then say, "Sure, you know when you're angry. I want you to know when you're irritated!"

What makes recognizing anxiety difficult is that instead of calling it anxiety we have come up with euphemisms for the word. Can you think of some? Here are a few:

Annoyed. Irritated. Worried. Disappointed.

Parents are remarkably good at using words like those on their kids. Perhaps you came home after your curfew and your parents met you at the door. They looked really stressed out but instead of saying that they were anxious they said something like this:

Parents: "We are so *disappointed* in you."

You: "You look anxious to me, not disappointed."

Parents: "We are disappointed."

You: "Sounds like you're anxious to me."

Parents: "We *are not anxious!* We're disappointed."

You: "Hmmmmm. Not really sure here. Looks and sounds a lot like anxiety to me."

Hopefully you said that last line under your breath or there would be real trouble.

Parents aren't the only ones guilty of this behavior. We use euphemisms at work as well. One of the words I hear most often is *confused*.

Russ:	"You guys look really worried over there."
Team:	"No—we're not worried at all. We are confused."
Russ:	"You sound anxious about your confusion."
Team:	"We're not anxious people, and resent that label. We are confused. If we stay confused for 3 more days we will be worried!"
Russ:	"Hmmmmm. What happens after you become worried? Will you get anxious?"
Team:	"The only way we're going to get anxious is if you keep on trying to call us anxious!"

What are some other substitute words you, your friends, your family and your co-workers use in place of anxiety? Maybe "stressed" or "under pressure or "frustrated." Maybe even the word "bored."

But wait! There are other ways we fail to recognize our anxiety for what it really is.

Here's one: sarcasm.

It's rampant in our society. Instead of recognizing the anxiety and just saying, "I am anxious" people will be sarcastic. They give backhanded compliments like, "Wow—you look better than I expected" or "Not bad for someone who didn't go to the Ivy League."

It's frightening when you think about it. Parents and teachers throw sarcastic comments at children all day long. They say, "Thanks for being on time" when the child is late. Or, at dinner more than one parent has said, "Good thing we don't live on a farm. The pigs would feel badly about themselves after seeing you eat."

Another one? Name calling.

What are some of the names you call yourself or others? Dumb. Stupid. Ignorant. Irresponsible. Thoughtless. You could make a long list.

There are a million ways that we can avoid dealing with our anxiety. You're probably ready to move to problem solving. Let's start by learning to recognize how full our anxiety buckets really are, and by adding a new Bucket Rule to our list.

RULE THREE
ANXIETY IS ONLY DANGEROUS WHEN IT IS STORED OR IGNORED!

Not too long ago I had a very important meeting with the secretary of state for the state of North Carolina. I landed at the Raleigh-Durham airport and it was raining. I'm from Montana, and while we're accustomed to having snow boots at the ready, we don't carry umbrellas. I was wearing my best suit, leather soled shoes, and a bright, beautiful silk tie.

"Oh great!" I thought to myself sarcastically. My bucket began to fill.

I grabbed my carry-on bag and went directly to the rental car garage. I am a gold member with some serious points and status with this rental car company, so in my mind I was expecting a friendly greeting, my name in lights and a car (upgrade, of course) waiting for me in a covered parking space.

You can probably guess what happened next. They had no record of my reservation. I finally produced a confirmation number and they presented me the keys to the only car that wasn't spoken for. It was a sub, sub compact and the air conditioning was broken. Despite my dream of a covered parking space that would preserve my suit, my tie and my dignity, it was of course parked in the back corner of their lot.

My bucket grew heavier.

It seemed to rain harder with every step I took across the lot. The leather soles on my shoes were soaked, and my suit wasn't just speckled—it was polka dot thanks to the size of the rain drops. I was cold and I was now in a hurry thanks to the unplanned delay. I threw open the door of the clown-sized car and threw my bags in the back seat.

At that moment, I began to consider that I just might be getting irritated.

I got downtown and couldn't find a parking place near the state capitol building, so I ended up parking seven or eight blocks away. I could have purchased a home with an attached garage in Raleigh for what I paid for half-day parking. I walked (stomped) to the building, through pouring rain, in sopping wet shoes, without an umbrella. The color from my silk tie was bleeding into my shirt. As I stepped through the doors, my friend and associate who I'd planned to meet was there waiting for me.

With concern in his voice I didn't hear, he said, "Russ, where have you been? We've been worried about you!"

My anxiety bucket exploded.

"Why don't you find a short pier and take a long walk!" I loudly suggested. "There is nothing good about today!"

He stood there stunned, wondering what on earth had just happened. Later, he watched me deliver a speech that wasn't as good as it could have been and again questioned what was wrong with me. All because I stored up my anxiety and ignored it until it was too late.

WHAT'S IN YOUR BUCKET?

(ANALYZE)

FOUR KEY QUESTIONS

Once we recognize our anxiety (sooner rather than later) we must analyze it. This is what we do in our **THINK** stage. We evaluate our feelings and consider responses that will help us get the outcomes we desire.

There are four questions that we must ask ourselves when we analyze our anxiety. They force us to stop and think which slows the anxiety dripping, or pouring, into our buckets.

1. **What is the target of my anxiety?**
2. **What triggered my anxiety?**
3. **How full is my bucket?**
4. **What do I want that I'm not getting?**

Which leads us to our next Bucket Rule.

RULE FOUR

> **REMEMBER THAT ANYTIME YOU ARE ANXIOUS IT'S BECAUSE YOU ARE NOT GETTING WHAT YOU WANT.**

When you're anxious ask yourself: "What do I want that I'm not getting?"

The value of that single question is incalculable. It allows you to focus on what you're not getting rather than expending time and energy fussing and carrying on about it.

Let me share a story.

In Billings Montana, the town where I live, there is an intersection that has been universally hated for decades: Grand Avenue and 17th Street West. Why? Because up until two weeks before I wrote this book, there was no left turn signal at that intersection.

If you were driving west down Grand, being in the left lane was the death knell to your commute. One or maybe two cars could turn left onto 17th Street West and then everyone who had wanted to go straight all along gets stuck at the intersection for at least two more light cycles. (Trust me—the right lane folks weren't about to slow down to let anyone in.)

Another important fact is that by the end of the average work day everybody's bucket is nearly full. But what do we all do after work? We get in our cars and drive home! No wonder we're having so much trouble on the roads. Our Anxiety Buckets are a public safety hazard!

One day last spring I was stuck in the left lane and I was doing a wonderful job alternating between suppression and projection of my anxiety. I needed to go straight in order to get home and I couldn't believe the City couldn't get it right.

After two cycles at that intersection I was the first one in line and I was ready to go. I'm no athlete but I know how to get moving after a red light. I was watching the lights and I could see the cross-traffic signals turning yellow. I was ready. A quick check of the crosswalk showed that I could proceed without putting any pedestrians at risk. The light turned green. As I was in the process of moving my foot from the brake to the gas pedal I heard a loud sound. I couldn't move my foot fast enough for the guy behind me: he was honking like a madman!

But I didn't hear just the horn. In my head I heard, "Hey stupid! There are only three colors on the light bar; two of the three mean go or go faster! Let's get moving!"

I hate being called stupid because, deep down inside, I'm afraid that I really am. Thus, in order to prove wasn't stupid, I proceeded to do something that seemed to prove the guy's point.

"All right buddy," I said out loud in my best Dirty Harry, go-ahead-and-make-my-day voice. "I give seminars for a living, and you are about to get one in slow!"

I inched off the line and then drove as slowly as my SUV would allow. If the driver to my right sped up, I sped up. If she slowed down, I slowed down. I was not going to let this guy who honked his horn get past me.

Now keep in mind this behavior gets people killed in cities all over America. But I didn't care. I was anxious, and as a result I engaged in unhealthy and irrational behavior.

Let's break this down by asking our four key questions:

1. What was the target of my anxiety?
In this case the target wasn't a "what" so much as a "who": the guy in the truck behind me.

2. What was the trigger?
The honk of a horn.

3. How full was my bucket?
Full to overflowing!

4. What did I want that I wasn't getting?
That one's not quite so easy, is it?

Without further analysis, you could say it was just that I wanted him to stop honking at me. But let's look deeper. Was he really a threat to me? No—I perceived that he was when I internalized the idea that he was calling me stupid, but really, there was nothing there. In fact, there would have been no problem at all if I hadn't created it. He just wanted to get home as much as I did.

Which takes us to another Bucket Rule.

RULE FIVE

WHEN A BEHAVIOR IS OUT OF PROPORTION TO THE TRIGGER - SOMETHING ELSE IS GOING ON. IN OTHER WORDS THE UNDERLYING CAUSE OF OUR ANXIETY NEEDS TO BE RECOGNIZED, ANALYZED, AND VERBALIZED.

This rule dictates that when we fly off the handle at the smallest provocation, there are other causes of our anxiety. It's time to look in our Anxiety Buckets and deal with the real threat.

When we "go off" that strongly it usually means that someone pulled one of our anxiety triggers. Every single one of us has at least one thing that will trigger us to anxiety no matter where we are or what we're doing.

What about the guy behind me at the intersection? I was his target, and his trigger was his perception that I lacked the lightning reflexes needed to ram my gas pedal to his satisfaction when the light changed. How full was his bucket? I think it's reasonable to assume it was at least as full of mine; in fact, it may have already spilled over the moment he pulled up behind me.

So let's pretend my seminar at Grand Avenue and 17th Street West didn't happen. Instead, I recognized my anxiety and just moved forward, allowing him to get around me if he felt strongly about it. I was able to keep my cool and not engage that other driver.

But where is the next danger zone? Home!

That's why at Cherry house we have Bucket Rule Number Six.

HOW TO EMPTY
YOUR BUCKET
(VERBALIZE)

RULE SIX

WHEN YOU KNOW YOUR BUCKET IS FULL (OR EVEN CLOSE TO BEING FULL) YOU MUST TELL PEOPLE.

A few years ago, when our kids were younger, I came home after speaking to a large group of people. It had gone spectacularly well, and I really felt I'd made a difference in their lives. As I headed up the front steps, I was still feeling that rush.

I burst through the door with enthusiasm and there was my beautiful wife, Colleen. She's an amazing person who is usually remarkably happy and upbeat. She's stood beside me through countless health challenges and she has been rock solid. But in that moment, she was STRESSED OUT.

Our daughter Emily, who was four or five at the time, had really been pressing her mother's buttons that day. My mate's Anxiety Bucket was ready to tip.

She looked me in the eye and said, "I am frustrated. I don't want you to fix my problem. Give me 20 minutes and I'll be ready to talk about it."

I replied a respectful, "Yes ma'am!" and took over the task of making dinner. After dinner Colleen was ready to talk. She had a plan in place and it worked out great. To this day, I'm still grateful she let me know that her bucket was full, that she didn't throw it at me and that she found a way to express herself in a healthy way.

It also opened the opportunity for any member of our family to announce "My bucket is full" and have the rest of us give him or her the time and space they need to exercise what I call a **secondary release of anxiety.**

RULE SEVEN

FIND AN EFFECTIVE, SAFE, SECONDARY RELEASE OF ANXIETY.

A secondary release of anxiety occurs when you can't go to the primary target to resolve how you're feeling in a healthy way. For instance, I can't go back to the guy who honked at me; I'll probably never see him again. (I certainly hope not.)

But let's go back to our pretend scenario, where I *didn't* provide him the slow seminar free of charge. Although his issue is resolved, mine isn't. I still have anxiety in my bucket, and even if I go home and get the all clear sign from my family, I'm still feeling agitated. So how do I release that anxiety?

It could be calling a good friend, or going for a long walk. Sometimes it's getting out in my garage building something (swinging a hammer is great therapy!). The goal is to burn up that negative energy so that you can think clearly, keep your options open and respond in a healthy way.

BUCKET EMPTYING STRATEGIES

Over the years, I have created Anxiety Bucket emptying strategies to help families, businesses and organizations. I would invite you to choose one strategy and practice it. As you master that principle, choose another and practice some more.

It's good to have more than one tool in your toolbox, as you may find yourself applying one tool in a given situation, then later using another tool later in the day with someone else.

Before you begin, remember: New skills don't feel "normal". It's a process that requires time and effort, and will feel uncomfortable at first. On that note, let me introduce anther Bucket Rule:

RULE EIGHT

BE KIND TO YOURSELF. NO ONE HANDLES ANXIETY PERFECTLY EVERY TIME!

You are going to fail occasionally when it comes to how you handle your anxiety. That's okay. Just dust off your Anxiety Bucket and begin again. If you stick with the strategy or technique - pretty soon it will stick to you!

STRATEGY ONE: THE CONTRACT

As you begin to recognize and analyze your anxiety, you will soon realize you will often need another person to help you safely empty your Anxiety Bucket. It should be someone you trust, the kind of person who, like my mentor, will understand the process. Once you both understand the expectations you may have, create a written agreement containing a version of the following language:

When my Anxiety Bucket is filling quickly, I will contact you and request your help in emptying it. I will ask you if you have time to help me, and provide a specific timeframe that allows you to know the time commitment and the urgency of the issue. Once we set a time to talk, I will share what's bothering me and ask you to help me to analyze what's in my bucket. I will respect your time and your feedback, listening to any thoughts you have to share.

When my Anxiety Bucket is brimming, and with our agreement in place, this is generally how a call to my mentor goes:

Russ: "Hi Ben. My bucket is full. Do you have time to help me empty it? I promise I'm not crazy—I'm safe and have cooled off. I am dealing with a difficult person at work and I need to find some ways to engage this guy. We're meeting again tomorrow, so I'd like to get this started by the end of the day."

Ben: "I'm glad you called. I'm committed for the next few hours. Would 4:00 pm work?"

Russ: "Perfect. I'll call then."

The key takeaways are:

- Make sure you have permission to start sharing
- Let them know what to expect in terms of a time commitment
- Be clear about the level of urgency

Also, you must be willing to reciprocate or, in other words, be willing to help that person empty their Anxiety Bucket when the time comes. Your relationship won't last long if it's totally one sided.

STRATEGY TWO: I FEEL...
WHEN YOU... BECAUSE...

Let's suppose for a moment you are feeling upset with someone. You know who they are and what they've done. You recognized your anxiety sooner and effectively analyzed it and you are ready to respond. Knowing where to begin, however, can be difficult. That's where this strategy comes into play.

We start by talking to the person *after* we have cooled off and use the formula below:

I feel: (describe the emotion)

when you: (objectively describe the behavior)

because: (describe what you want that you are not getting)

The goal is to tell that person how you feel, what triggered your feelings and the reason you are talking to them (what you want). I like this formula because although it does not solve the problem, it gets the issue out on the table and allows a reasonable discussion to begin.

I'll share a classic example from marriage counseling. Imagine a couple sitting in a counselor's office to work out some issues.

Norma:	"John golfs all the time. Will you tell him to not golf so much? It is so annoying."
John:	"I like golf. It's my only escape, and I won't give it up."
Norma:	"I see how it is. You would rather golf than be with me!"
John:	"I can't win. You're always complaining about me playing golf! Sheesh!"

At this point in the conversation the counselor introduces our formula.

Counselor:	"Let's try this again. Norma, will you please phrase your issue with John playing golf by using: I feel, when you, because?"
Norma:	"Okay. John, I feel sad when you golf all the time because you're golfing!"
Counselor:	"That's a good first try. Now, improve the because portion of your statement. Tell him what you want that you're not getting."
Norma:	"Oh, okay. (Takes a moment to calm down.) John, I feel sad when you are golfing because I would like to spend time with you."

As you can imagine, John stares at his wife, slack-jawed. He just learned that the real issue isn't golf; it was spending more time together. His wife was actually showing that she enjoyed his company and would like to have more of it!

Once the issue is on the table, the couple has something concrete to focus on and work towards. It's measurable, and can usually be accomplished if both parties are willing to work at it.

Now let me give you another example, something that I've seen countless times in companies and organizations of every shape and size:

Harold comes to work ten minutes late nearly every day. His tardiness keeps you from getting your work done because you have to cover for him. Worse yet, your boss gets on you for always being behind for the first hour of each and every day. Here's the kicker: your boss knows about the behavior but won't discipline him. Instead, she distributes Harold's work—and the blame for being behind--on the rest of the team.

How many Anxiety Buckets are full because of situations just like this one? How much anxiety is being suppressed or misplaced as a result?

Now, you can't say "I feel anxious because you don't care about me" to Harold. You must talk about behaviors that have led you to believe that they do not care about you.

Is the following "I feel, when you, because" statement specific enough?

You: "Harold, I am frustrated because you don't take your job seriously."

I hope you saw that the above statement is still incomplete. It doesn't tell Harold what you are upset about, and it certainly doesn't tell him what you want. In fact, Harold is likely to see it as an attack on his character. Instead, consider this:

You: "Harold, I feel angry. When you were ten minutes late this morning, I had to cover your responsibilities and mine. Because of it, my own work won't be turned in on time."

Phew! You've told him how you feel, what triggered it and the reason you are talking to him. No slamming drawers or name-calling. The real issue has been revealed, and the opportunity to discuss it more completely.

What happens if you use the formula and Harold doesn't change? Think through that possibility ahead of time. What will you do if you still can't get what you need? Determining your "Plan B" (talking to your supervisor, going to Human Resources, refusing to do Harold's work anymore, seeking a new job, etc.) allows you to avoid being trapped in any of the five unhealthy responses to anxiety and puts you solidly in control of what comes next.

STRATEGY THREE: CREATING AN ANXIETY POLICY

I feel, when you, because gets the issue on the table. *Plan B* helps you think of alternatives so that you don't get stuck. Getting together with your family or the people you work with to formulate an ***anxiety policy*** makes problem solving easier to start and resolve.

An anxiety policy describes the rules for how anxiety will be dealt with when it is out in the open. We've all seen anxiety turn into a verbal or emotional bloodletting, which tells us that getting the anxiety out is not enough. You must also agree far ahead of time what to do and how to respond when the anxiety is verbalized.

I strongly suggest that some of the hard-and-fast guidelines within your anxiety policy include:

- There can be no putdowns, discounts or name-calling
- The person who is anxious must not sit on or suppress their anxiety
- Whenever possible and appropriate, there should be a cooling down period between the tripping of the anxiety trigger and the discussion
- Only one person speaks at a time
- There must be frequent pauses to allow listening

STRATEGY FOUR: ANXIOUS CHILD OF THE WEEK

In our family we have an award. We call it the "Anxious Child of the Week" prize.

Surprised? Most people are when they hear about it, because they immediately visualize someone who yells the loudest or maybe intimidates other members of our family. On occasion, people will have the overwhelming strong desire to call child protective services on me as they believe it's our way of shaming someone.

The more negative their response, the more fun I have talking about it with them! You see, it shows how quickly our negative association with the word "anxiety" dominates our lives. So imagine the look on their faces when I explain how our kids get to win the prize.

Since our kids have been little we have consistently asked the following two questions every night at the dinner table. First, we ask them what was hard about their day. Then we ask them what they did to work through that hard thing. We start with our youngest and work our way up. Let me share an experience we had with Emily a few years ago.

Russ: "What was hard today and what did you do about it?"

Emily: "I was doing a math paper and needed help. I was getting frustrated, so I raised my hand. My teacher never saw my hand and I got more and more frustrated."

Russ: "So, what did you do about it?"

Emily: "Well Dad, I grabbed my paper and walked up to his desk and asked him for help!"

From the example above you can see that at a young age Emily was able to recognize, analyze, and verbalize her anxiety. She found a healthy response instead of falling prey to the Fearsome Five. She felt great and I felt even better!

Now that they're older, our kids have begun to ask Colleen and I the same questions. It's given us the chance to model and discuss anxiety as a healthy emotion that can provide healthy results. Dinner became (and still is!) is a great and very safe place for all of us to empty our Anxiety Buckets.

You can have the same experience at home, at work, or within any organization. At first, people will think you're crazy because they have the same negative association with anxiety as you did before trying these techniques out. But they will catch on quickly and make a fun game out of what used to be a touchy subject.

To make it easy, I've included an outline of the Anxious Child Award guidelines.

ANXIOUS CHILD OF THE WEEK GUIDELINES

1. Establish an anxiety policy
2. Review the policy
3. Announce that you are instituting The Anxious Child (parent, employee, volunteer) of the Week Award
4. Explain that it is NOT awarded to the person who:
   - is the most dysfunctional
   - yells the loudest
   - gives the best cold shoulder
   - shames or guilts others into compliance
5. Explain that it goes to the person who got anxious about something and managed it in a healthy way that produced a measurable outcome Examples include:
   - five fewer arguments this week
   - a new system or procedure that produced a good result
   - refined systems that speed up a process
   - a new way to do something that removes a "bottleneck"
   - an improved relationship
6. Show the award. It could be a t-shirt, trophy, certificate or even gift card
7. Set up a time every week to give the award
8. Make sure everyone is able to hear what was improved or changed
9. Make it part of your Sunday family dinner or weekly staff meeting
10. Stick to it and it will stick to you! Don't give up! You can do it!

WHAT YOU'VE LEARNED

The Anxiety Bucket is provoking, challenging, sometimes scary, often exciting and always powerful. Congratulations on making it through; hopefully you'll soon learn the rewards you'll reap as a result of applying these principles will be well worth the time and effort you devote to this process.

You now know my story, the reason I wrote this book. I thought I was over my anxiety when it came to my cancer, but I had only repressed it. When it roared to life in an undesirable way, I was fortunate to have a few caring people around me to get me back on my feet and pointed in the right direction.

You are now on a path of your own. You have the tools to see the anxiety in and around you that is hidden plain sight. Unresolved anxiety is a silent killer of relationships, businesses, ideas, and self esteem. Shine the light into some of the dark corners of your life and deal with anxiety you may be feeling.

You have learned that anxiety is a positive emotion that can help us achieve positive outcomes in our lives. It is our teacher, our friend and euphoric in its own way. It is normal to feel anxiety and necessary to work through!

You learned where anxiety got a bad name. You can now recognize it in your behaviors and the behaviors of those around you. You have the ability to change anxiety's reputation in your life and in the lives of people you love and serve.

You learned about the anxiety cycle, and now know that if you aren't paying attention, the Fearsome Five can wreak havoc on your emotions, your health, and your relationships. You must think in order to cancel the debilitating effects of unresolved anxiety.

You have a new paradigm for anxiety—the Anxiety Bucket. Recognize your anxiety sooner, then analyze it. Remember that life is a team sport and there are good friends and loved ones who will help you safely empty your bucket.

You may wonder whether or not I still get anxious. The answer is: absolutely.

Life can be unfair and at times it can feel unjust. I wrote this book and published it in response to yet another life threatening medical situation that I don't deserve but had to work through. I have been given less than a day to live on more than one occasion. It's never easy to hear, but it taught me an incredible lesson.

The first time I was told that I wasn't expected to live another day was in 1988. I remember the two thoughts that filled my mind after the doctor pronounced my doom. I could think of nothing else:

1. Do the people around me know that I love them?
2. Did I make a difference in their lives?

Since then I have learned to love more people than just the ones around me. I love people and they are filled with limitless potential. No life has to be wasted or unfulfilled. I have travelled all over and I keep finding reasons to love people more, not less.

You matter to me. I want you to engage life and try even when you feel you have failed. Most failures aren't terminal. I have learned that if I can breathe, if there is life still in me, I have a chance. I yearn for one more day to find one more person to make a difference for. Every day another person that needs help appears, almost magically, and they give me a chance to make a difference in their life.

I know that the same can be true for you. Will you join me?

I sincerely thank you for spending time with me by learning about The Anxiety Bucket. It means so much to me that you've taken the time out of your busy schedule to read my book and follow my advice. I am honored to serve you. I hope these principles, strategies, and tips make a true difference in your life and in the lives of those you love.

Russ Cherry

P.S. On the following pages I have included an excerpt from my upcoming book "Dealing With Difficult People". I hope you enjoy it!

COMING SOON!

DEALING WITH DIFFICULT PEOPLE

Most of us deal with one or more difficult person every day. They're not all difficult all of the time, but often enough to send us up the wall and interfere with what we have to do. There are useful techniques for dealing with people like that. This book is based on the course I teach on just that subject — how to deal with difficult people. It isn't a treatise on abnormal psychology, and it may not improve your love life. But I hope it helps you cope with the people who take advantage of you and drive you crazy.

The amazing thing is that everybody knows difficult people, but nobody is one — or at least nobody thinks so. That may be correct. It is important to remember that even wonderful people like you and me can occasionally be difficult. Very difficult people are not that common. Only ten percent of the population fits this special category. At times it seems like more! Therefore, the place to begin is in identifying the characteristics of difficult people. You will be pleased to discover that there really is a difference between difficult people and delightful human beings like you and me. There are five characteristics that distinguish the difficult ones.

CHARACTERISTICS OF DIFFICULT PEOPLE

CHARACTERISTIC ONE: PREDICTABLE ABRASIVE BEHAVIOR

The first characteristic is that these folks have a predictable, abrasive style of behavior. You can count on them. They'll never let you down. If you're late to work on Monday and miss their Monday morning groaning, moaning, and complaining, don't worry... they'll be back Tuesday doing the same thing they did on Monday! They do not have a bad Monday -- they have a bad August. When they say last year was bad, they mean every single day. The style is so predictable that you are more surprised when their behavior is acceptable than when it's not. If the difficult person arrives cheerful and sunny one morning, you comment on it. But don't worry, the sunshine will go away. By lunch, the person's behavior will be back to its usual negative pattern.

The key word here is abrasive. By "abrasive" I mean anything that gets on your nerves. Many people think that abrasive means yelling, screaming, and hollering. That is certainly abrasive, but the word means more than that. It means any behavior that really bothers you. Yelling, screaming, and hollering get on one's nerves, but then there are the people who say nothing, absolutely nothing. You talk to them and they mutter, "Um, um, uh hum." Or, they simply nod their head. They do not yell; they simply don't say anything. And they can make you go crazy!

Another type of abrasive behavior is what I call the "nauseatingly nice guy." Nauseatingly nice guys have no mind of their own. In meetings, a colleague makes a proposal and the nice guy says, "Way to go, Bob."

Mary objects to the idea and the nauseatingly nice person says, "Know what you mean, Mary. Good point there."

Bob says, "I thought you agreed with me." "Well, I do." Says the nauseatingly nice guy. Mary says, "I thought you agreed with me." "Well, I do." He says again

Finally somebody says to the nice guy, "I think you are kind of two-faced." And the nauseatingly nice guy replies with, "You're right, I probably am."

The first common thread among difficult people is that they consistently do something you find abrasive.

CHARACTERISTIC TWO: EXPERIENCED AS DIFFICULT BY MOST PEOPLE

The second characteristic is that most people find them difficult. The key word is "most". Nearly everybody finds these people difficult, not just you. If you ask someone, "What do you think about her?" that person would probably reply, "She drives us all nuts!". Managers complain about difficult folks. "He was in our department this year. Don't you think somebody else ought to have him next year?" We tend to move these types around in self-defense! Thus, regardless of specific experiences, people usually agree with you that these folks are difficult. That's Characteristic Two.

CHARACTERISTIC THREE: KEEP BLAME AND RESPONSIBILITY OUTSIDE OF SELF

Third, difficult people carefully keep the blame and responsibility for problems outside themselves. Recognizing this characteristic is the key to understanding difficult people. If anything goes wrong, in their minds it is necessarily your fault, or certainly somebody else's. They are likely to say,

"It's not my fault; nobody told me." "That's not the way you explained it." "You got here too early." "You didn't send enough information." "This is one messed-up place." "Have you looked in the mirror lately?" From their perspective, you caused the problem; it's all your fault. The fact is that they think and perceive differently from you. They do not see the world as you see it. It's important to look at the world through their eyes. Their first conclusion is that it is the world that's out of sync, not them. Line these folks up to march with a thousand other people, and they would be the one with their left foot out of step. However, they would say to themselves, "Look at all these fools — everybody is out of step but me."

In addition, they see life as one big problem after another. That is all life is to them — one big problem. Furthermore, they are convinced that you caused the problem. It's your fault, so you should fix it. They give it to you, blame you for it — and when you begin to deal with it, they resist cooperating with you. When you try to deal with the problem, you discover that you are getting no cooperation at all. The reason these people resist working toward resolution is that *they do not believe that problems can be solved*. They have no clear problem-solving strategy or procedure. Their way of solving problems is to blame someone else for them.

That is a pretty good "dodge" if you don't know how to fix the problem. I've known mangers who have been doing that for years. They tend to say that their employees are no good. Instead of looking inside and saying, "Maybe it's my fault," they blame the people they manage. That's one management style.

There's a little poem that goes like this:

When in worry, when in doubt Run in circles, scream and shout.

If you don't know what you're doing, scream and shout about how stupid the people around you are. Blame everybody else. Never look inside. That's a clas- sic difficult person's response.

While difficult people tend to blame others, you and I tend to blame ourselves. Thus we can be called "neurotics". Don't be offended at being called neurotic. When I use the word, which has many meanings, I mean a person who tends to place the blame excessively on himself.

Neurotics say, "It's my fault." "I messed up." "I'd be glad to fix it." We even take responsibility when the problem at hand isn't of our making.

For example, standing in a line at the theater, a guy steps on my foot, and I say, "Excuse me, sir. I feel really bad about this. If you will kindly lift your heel I would gladly move my foot. I'm just so embarrassed that I carelessly left my foot there in the first place. I hope you can find it in your heart to forgive me." Stupid, but I have done comparable things. What am I doing? I am taking re- sponsibility and accepting blame for someone else's behavior.

Or say that two neurotics start to go through a door at the same time. One says to the other, "Excuse me, you go first."

Says the second neurotic to the first, "No, you go first." Replies the first neurotic to the second, "No, you go first."

If it's raining, they'll drown before they get through that door.

We neurotics just "nice" each other to death. We blame ourselves far, far too much. Notice what this sets up in connection with difficult people. The difficult person and you get together, you have this enormous conflict, nothing is resolved, you are both mad, and you go home thinking, "Wish I had said this." "Can't believe I didn't say that." "I must have been a fool and an idiot to not say that." While you're at home flogging yourself, the difficult person is home saying about you the same things you're saying about yourself. Both of you agree that you are an idiot! This is the common ground that you have.

The trouble arises when you and the difficult person get together. Unless you do something about it, the problem will wind up in your court every time — and stay there. Difficult people are what I call "sellers". They love to sell problems. Folks like you and me, we are "buyers" - we love to buy problems. If someone wants to turn us neurotics on, he only needs to say that something can not be done. We jump up and say, "We will do that in three days!" "No way we can't do that!" You and I like to solve problems. We are problem solvers. When a difficult person comes along and says, "It can't be done" we automatically buy the problem. We take it and run with it. They are sellers. We are buyers. That MUST stop.

Therefore, the purpose of this book is to get the problem back into the difficult person's court and keep it there. Difficult people do not bring you only the problems that the two of you share — they bring you their problems as well. They want you to be responsible for their decisions, their work, and their results. They want to blame you for anything that goes wrong in the organization. They want to keep the blame outside of themselves. You and I tend to put the blame on ourselves. The third hallmark of difficult people is that they place blame and responsibility outside of themselves.

CHARACTERISTIC FOUR: ROBBERS OF TIME AND ENERGY

Difficult people are robbers of time and energy. A minute with these people is like a day with anybody else. When you are with one of them, you have only one thought in mind — how to get away. "Good to see you. Hope to see you again in the year 2080." You say to yourself when you are with her, "This woman makes me sick!" "She is a pain in the neck!" "She's killing me!"

And you're right. Notice what happens to your body physiologically when you are with these people. You feel tired. Your back tightens up. Your stomach tightens up. Your knees begin to shake. Your head begins to feel tense. These folks really wear you out. They are robbers of time and energy.

They do not even have to be present to affect you. Someone can simply mention their name. If you are walking down the hallway and they are coming toward you, you will hide in the bathroom to get out of their way. You do not want to be with them. They rob you of energy. They rob you of time.

CHARACTERISTIC FIVE: BEHAVIOR OUT OF PROPORTION TO THE PROBLEM

Fifth, the behavior of difficult people is out of proportion to the problem. The behavior is exaggerated. I call it the "Henny-Penny, Chicken Little Syndrome". They get hit in the head with an acorn and the whole sky is falling. They come rushing up to you and say, "You wouldn't believe, wouldn't believe, wouldn't believe...". You don't even know what the problem is yet, and you are already in a panic. When you find out what is wrong, it is so small in comparison to the way they present it that you get angry with them for sending you into panic-mode.

As you can see, difficult people seem to be driven to keep you off balance and away from problem solving. And of course, they are determined that you end up with the problem, whatever it is, in your court. Remember, the behavior of difficult people is out of proportion to the problem.

SUMMARY

To summarize the five characteristics of difficult people:

1. They have a predictable, abrasive style of behavior.
2. They are experienced as difficult and abrasive by nearly everybody.
3. They keep the blame and responsibility for problems outside themselves.
4. They are robbers of time and energy.
5. Their behavior is out of proportion to the problem.

Sometimes, a wonderful person like you and me says that he knows someone he considers difficult — that is, something about the person's chronic behavior is driving you crazy (Characteristic One), but the person he perceives as difficult does not have all five characteristics. Please note that once an individual places the blame and responsibility outside of their ability to impact (Characteristic Three), he also has the other four. Once he stats blaming you, you find it ex- hausting to be with him (Characteristic Four). Then you begin to notice that nearly everybody feels about this person the way you do (Characteristic Two). So now we are up to four characteristics out of five, and since most people with the first four characteristics will exaggerate the seriousness of what is going on, they automatically have the fifth characteristic. Bingo, five out of five.

Do difficult people recognize themselves? No, they don't have a clue! They do not see themselves this way at all. Difficult people rarely take my seminar designed to deal with them. "Don't need it," they say. "Nothing's wrong with me." They send other people to the seminar!

Difficult people cannot afford to see themselves the way they are. Seeing themselves accurately would be far too painful. Believe it or not, they are taking care of themselves psychologically the only way they know how. Unfortunately, it is abrasive. Yet for difficult people to see themselves as they are is almost impossible.

Sometimes someone in my class says, "You know, when I read those characteristics, I realize I have some similar characteristics, and that scares me. I think I may be difficult. Do you think I'm difficult?" I always respond, "You probably can be difficult on any given day — all of us can — but you do not fit the category of a difficult person because the moment you look inside, you eliminate yourself. Difficult people do not look inside. They never seriously ask, 'Could it be me?'".

One other thing about difficult people is that most of them have a physical or emotional problem that is chronic. They have a bad back, a bad leg, a bad toe, a bad heart, whatever — something is bad, and it is chronic. Or they have a disease. The doctors do not know what it is yet, but they are working on it at the Center for Disease Control in Atlanta and someday there will be a cure for it. Meanwhile, they suffer, but not in silence.

So who are the difficult people in your life, and what can you do about them? Before answering those questions, it is first necessary to examine the four pitfalls in dealing with difficult people.

Made in the USA
Las Vegas, NV
02 May 2022